Pure & Simple

SPIRITUALS

Arranged for Easy Piano by Carol Tornquist

D1733175

Now you can play the music from church that you love to hear and sing with the *Pure & Simple* series. Each book features lyrics, suggested fingerings, phrasing, pedal markings, and easy-to-read notation. The solo piano arrangements, which use familiar harmonies and rhythms, will put your favorite melodies at your fingertips quickly and easily.

This volume features spirituals, a genre which began in the fields of the southern United States where slaves combined the rhythms and tonalities of their native Africa with their new knowledge of the Bible. They improvised spirituals throughout the 18th and 19th centuries, combining hymn tunes and Scripture passages with elements such as "call and response" and syncopation. Spirituals provided the foundation for blues, jazz, and gospel music, and continue to be a rich part of today's musical culture.

Alfred

CONTENTS

DEEP RIVER

Traditional Spiritual
Arranged by Carol Tornquist

Slowly and freely

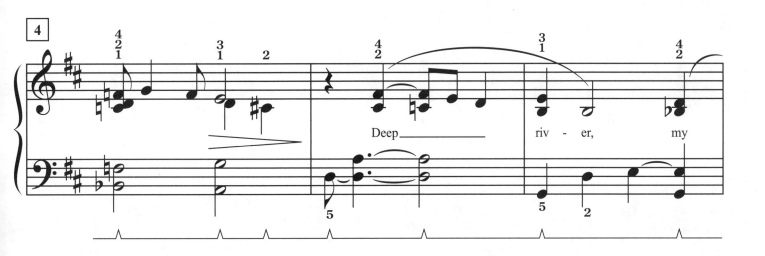

riv - er, Lord, I want to cross o - ver in - to camp - ground.

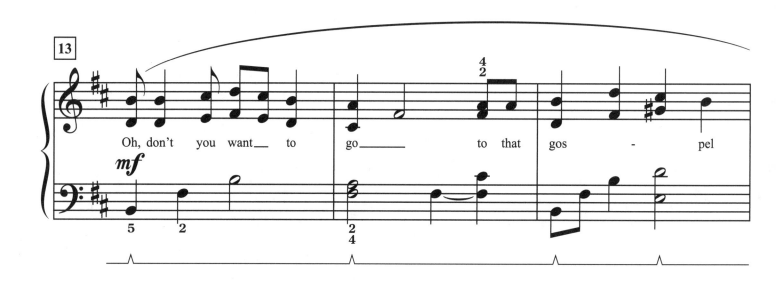

Oh, don't you want___ to go_____ to that gos - pel

feast, that prom - ised land___ where all___ is

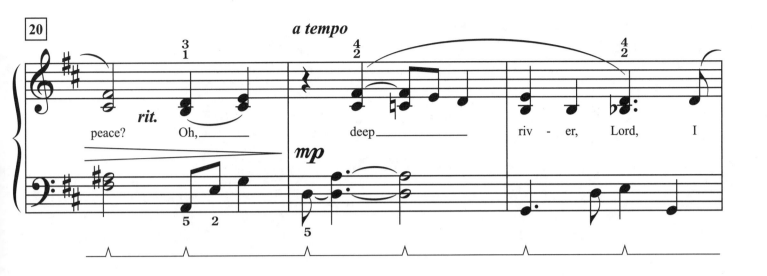

peace? Oh,_____ deep_____ riv - er, Lord, I

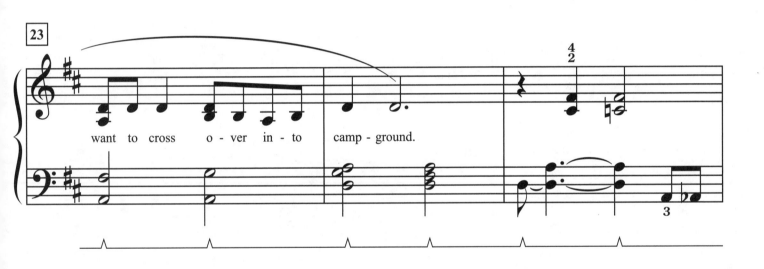

want to cross o - ver in - to camp - ground.

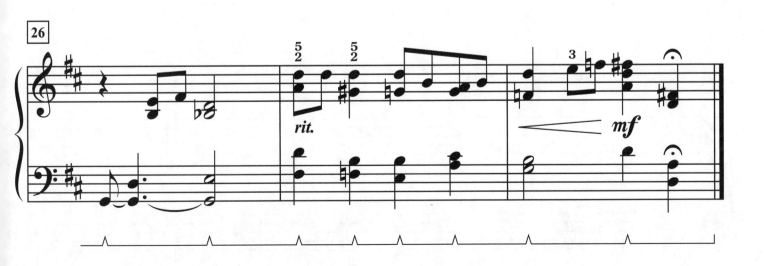

AIN'T-A THAT GOOD NEWS

Traditional Spiritual
Arranged by Carol Tornquist

Moderately, in two

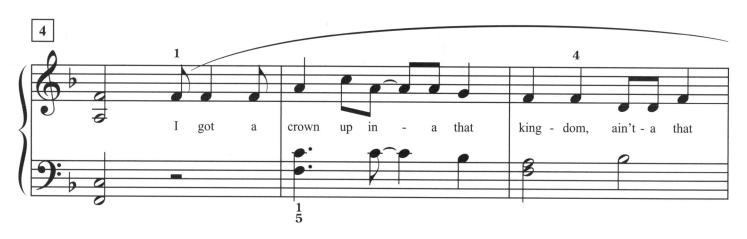

good news?

I got a crown up in-a that

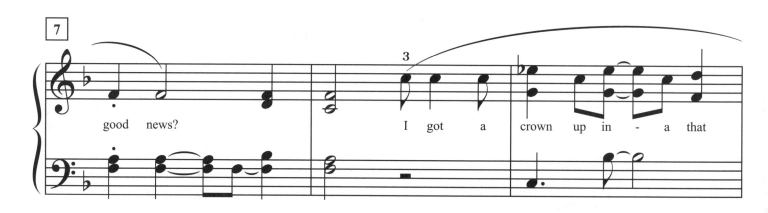

I got a crown up in-a that

EZEKIEL SAW THE WHEEL

Traditional Spiritual
Arranged by Carol Tornquist

Moderately fast

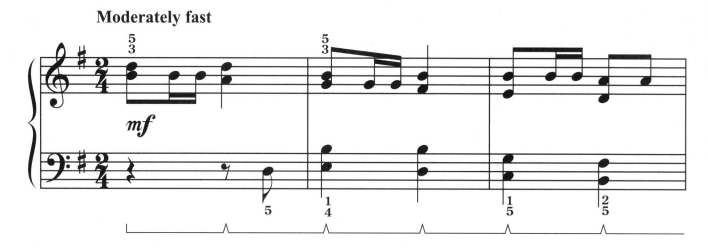

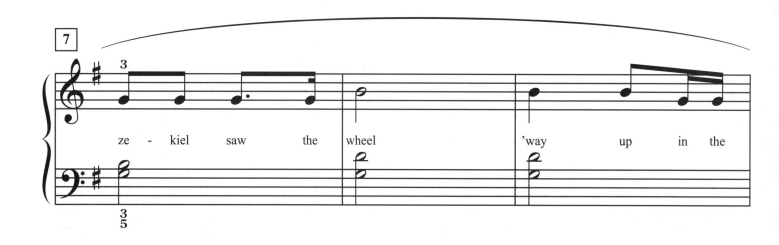

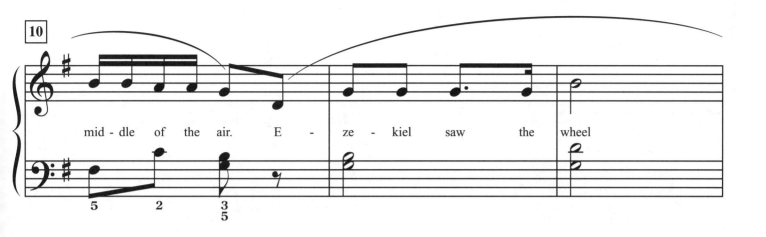

mid - dle of the air. E - ze - kiel saw the wheel

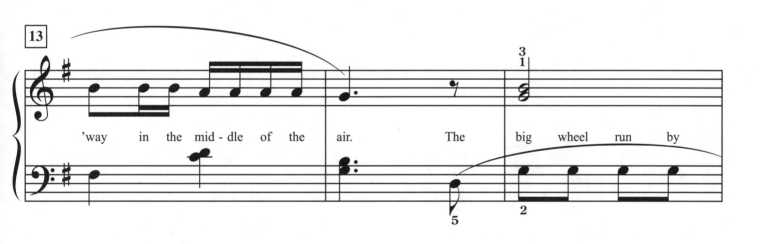

'way in the mid - dle of the air. The big wheel run by

faith, the lit - tle wheel run by the grace of God; a

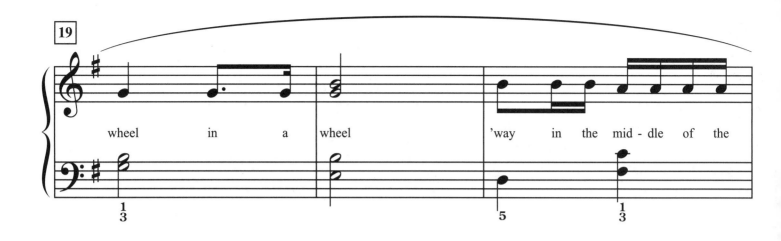

wheel in a wheel 'way in the mid - dle of the

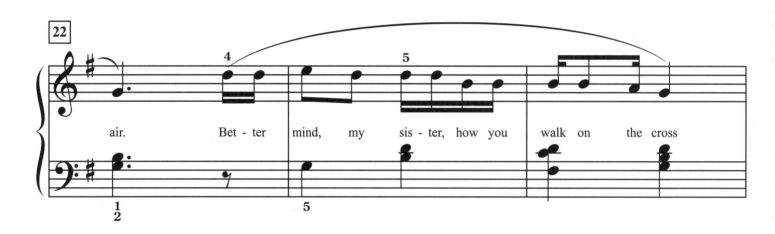

air. Bet - ter mind, my sis - ter, how you walk on the cross

'way in the mid - dle of the air. Your foot might slip and your

soul be lost 'way in the mid - dle of the air. E -

Every Time I Feel the Spirit

Traditional Spiritual
Arranged by Carol Tornquist

Ev - 'ry time I____ feel the Spir - it____ mov - ing in my heart,____ I will pray;_____ ev - 'ry

time I____ feel the Spir - it____ mov - ing in my heart,__ I will pray;_____ ev - 'ry

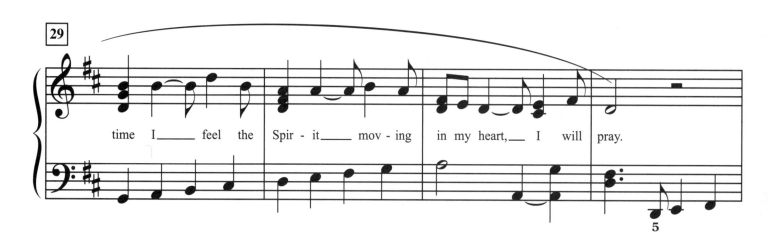

time I____ feel the Spir - it____ mov - ing in my heart,__ I will pray.

(no rit.) ***f***

GIVE ME THAT OLD-TIME RELIGION

Traditional Spiritual
Arranged by Carol Tornquist

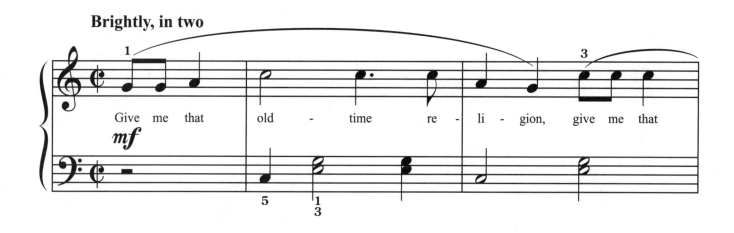

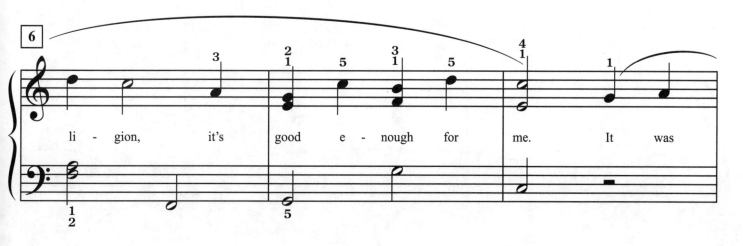

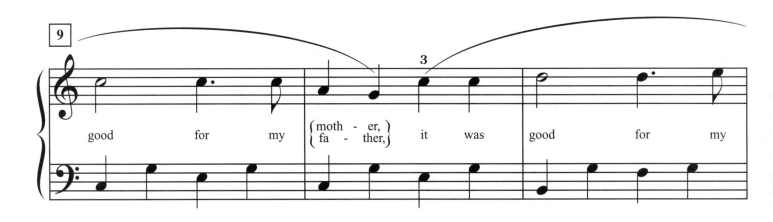

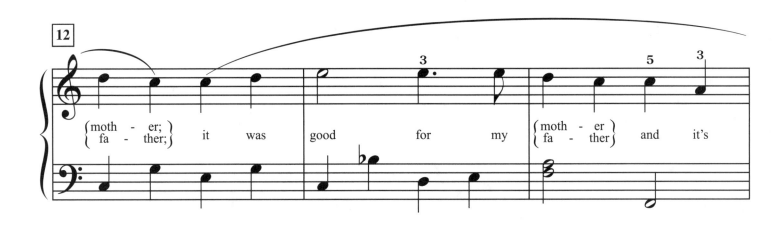

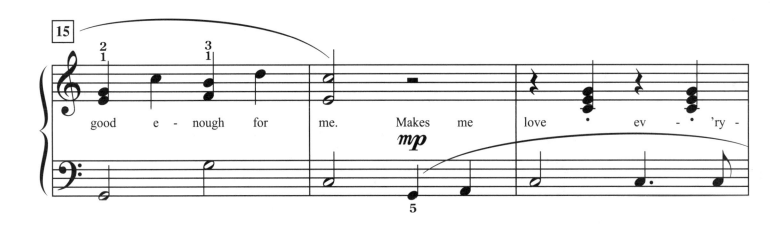

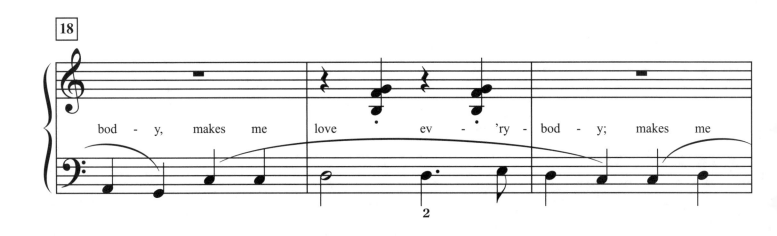

Go Down, Moses

Traditional Spiritual
Arranged by Carol Tornquist

Slowly, in two

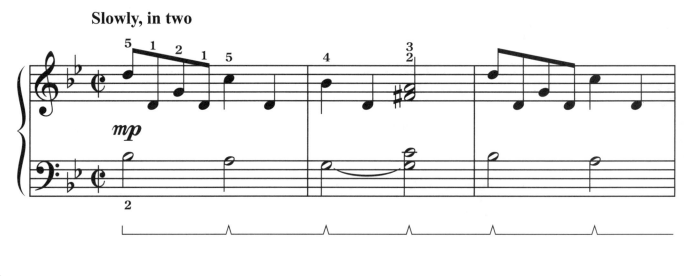

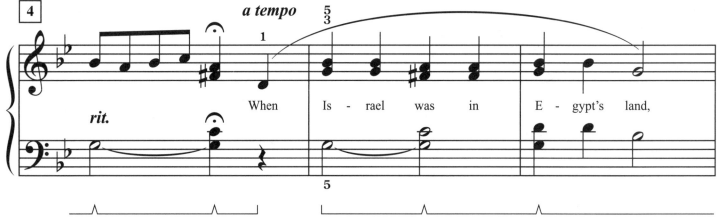

When Is - rael was in E - gypt's land,

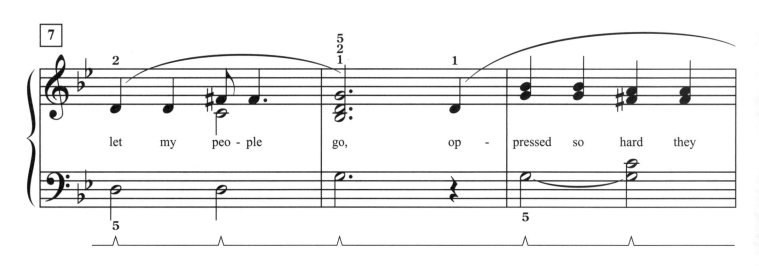

let my peo - ple go, op - pressed so hard they

GO, TELL IT ON THE MOUNTAIN

Traditional Spiritual
Arranged by Carol Tornquist

HE'S GOT THE WHOLE WORLD
IN HIS HANDS

Traditional Spiritual
Arranged by Carol Tornquist

I'VE GOT PEACE LIKE A RIVER

Traditional Spiritual
Arranged by Carol Tornquist

34

LET US BREAK BREAD TOGETHER

Traditional Spiritual
Arranged by Carol Tornquist

LITTLE DAVID, PLAY ON YOUR HARP

Traditional Spiritual
Arranged by Carol Tornquist

play on your harp, hal - le - lu! Lit - tle Da - vid,

play on your harp, hal - le - lu, hal - le - lu! Lit - tle Da - vid,

play on your harp, hal - le - lu! Lit - tle

Da - vid was a shep - herd boy; he

lu! Lit - tle, Da - vid, play on your harp, hal - le -

lu! _____

MICHAEL, ROW THE BOAT ASHORE

Traditional Spiritual
Arranged by Carol Tornquist

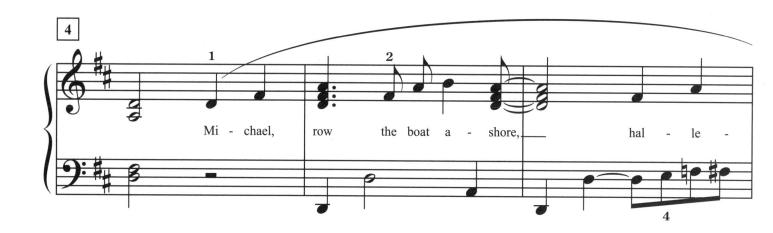

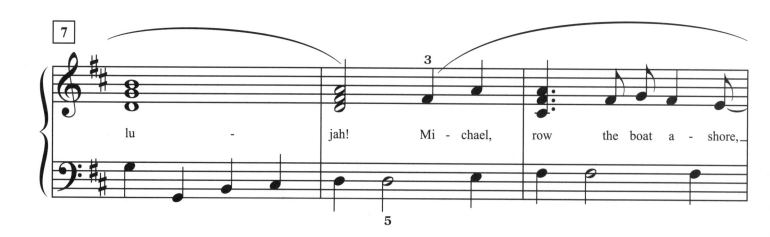

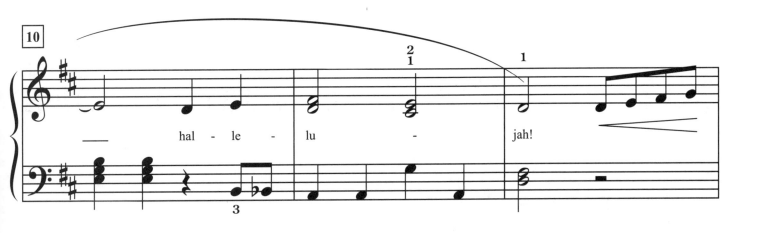

hal - le - lu - jah!

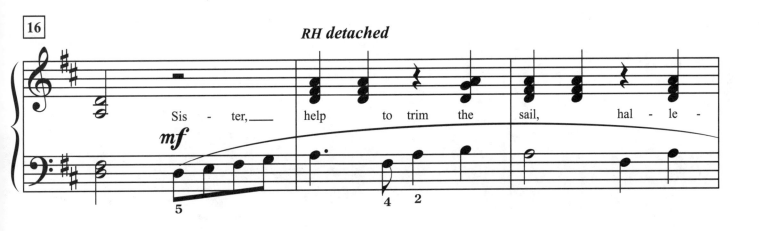

RH detached

Sis - ter,___ help to trim the sail, hal - le -

lu - jah! Sis - ter, help to trim the

sail, hal - le - lu - jah!

My Lord, What a Morning!

Traditional Spiritual
Arranged by Carol Tornquist

NOBODY KNOWS
THE TROUBLE I'VE SEEN

Traditional Spiritual
Arranged by Carol Tornquist

Sometimes I Feel Like a Motherless Child

Traditional Spiritual
Arranged by Carol Tornquist

Slowly and deliberately

SWING LOW, SWEET CHARIOT

Traditional Spiritual
Arranged by Carol Tornquist

THERE IS A BALM IN GILEAD

Traditional Spiritual
Arranged by Carol Tornquist

THIS LITTLE LIGHT OF MINE

Traditional Spiritual
Arranged by Carol Tornquist

Brightly

This lit-tle light of mine, I'm gon-na let it shine.

This lit-tle light of mine, I'm gon-na let it shine, let it

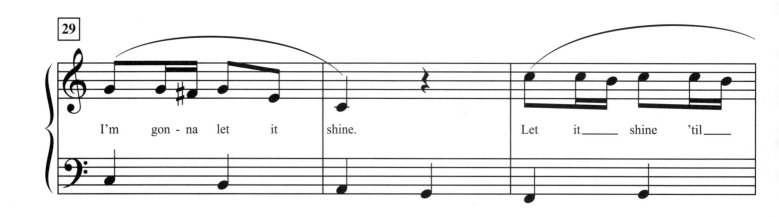

I'm gon - na let it shine. Let it___ shine 'til___

Je - sus comes, I'm gon - na let it shine, let it

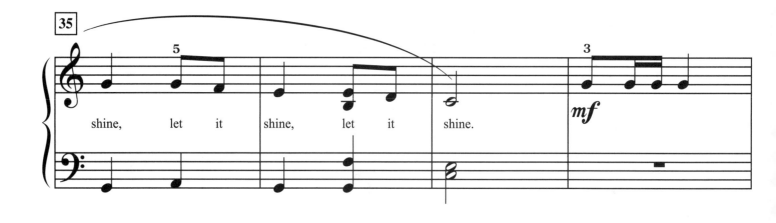

shine, let it shine, let it shine. *mf*

WE SHALL OVERCOME

Traditional Spiritual
Arranged by Carol Tornquist

Wayfaring Stranger

Traditional Spiritual
Arranged by Carol Tornquist

WE ARE CLIMBING JACOB'S LADDER

Traditional Spiritual
Arranged by Carol Tornquist

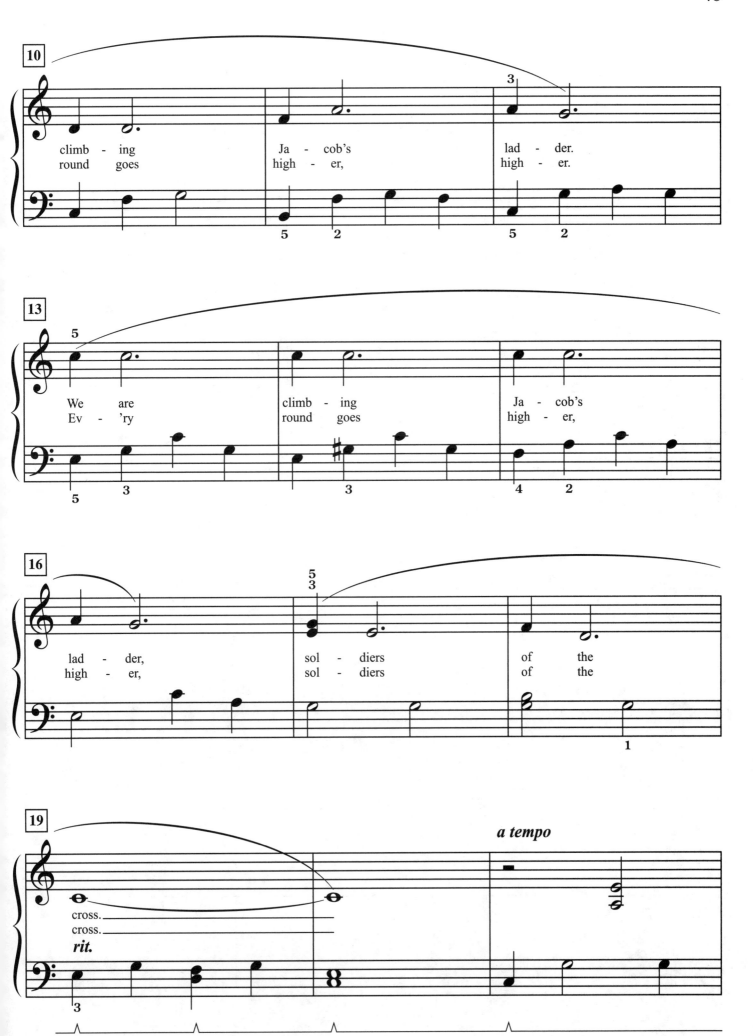

WERE YOU THERE?

Traditional Spiritual
Arranged by Carol Tornquist

Moderately slow, with expression

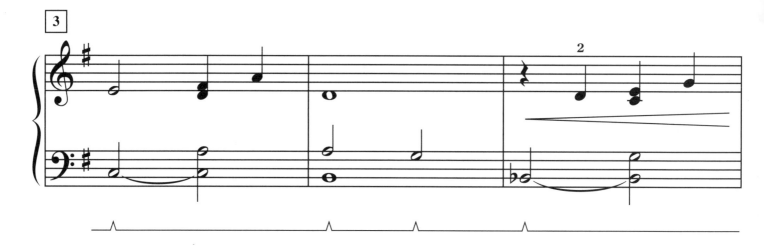

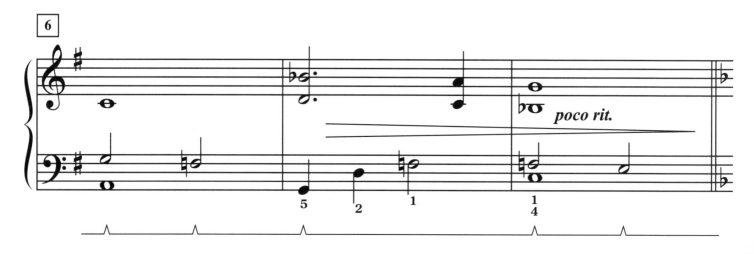